The Truth About
CAT PEOPLE

ISBN: 978-1-68088-341-1

▉ and Blue Mountain Press are registered in U.S. Patent and Trademark Office. Certain trademarks are used under license.

Printed in China.
Second Printing: 2021

✿ This book is printed on recycled paper.

This book is printed on paper that has been specially produced to be acid free (neutral pH) and contains no groundwood or unbleached pulp. It conforms with the requirements of the American National Standards Institute, Inc., so as to ensure that this book will last and be enjoyed by future generations.

Blue Mountain Arts, Inc.
P.O. Box 4549, Boulder, Colorado 80306

The Truth About
CAT PEOPLE

Jo Renfro

Blue Mountain Press™
Boulder, Colorado

Cat People
are patient...

...and they love surprises.

Cat People
prefer clutter-free
surfaces.

They
climb trees...

...and wear cat hats
when they read.

Cat People are
good at sharing.

They never throw
away boxes.

Cat People
have furniture
that is well-loved.

Maybe Cat People
are a little crazy,
but good crazy,
because they get
to hang out with cats.
And cats are cool.

Cat People are
experts on fur
on their clothes,
on their furniture,
and... well, you know.

MEOW
MEOW
MEOW
MEOW
MEOW
MEOW
MEOW
MEOW
MEOW
MEOW
MEOW
MEOW
MEOW
MEOW

Are you hungry perhaps?

And they are intuitive too.

MEOW

Cat People leave
the curtains open and
let the sunshine in.

And they love
to laugh.

Cat People
are never lonely.

Cat People know that
cats make their homes
feel warm and fuzzy...

...and that the purr
is mightier than the claw.

They also understand
that everyone needs
a little time to themselves.

But no matter what,
Cat People love cats,
and cats love them.

About the Author

Jo Renfro is a freelance writer and illustrator with a passion for mixing color, pattern, and whimsy in her somewhat quirky, often amusing, and always upbeat work.

She enjoys using her sense of humor developed from raising three kids, several dogs, numerous cats, and a potbellied pig named Matilda to create pieces that are lightheartedly inspirational.

Her love of the outdoors, animals, and her amazing kids is often reflected in her work.

A lifelong Kansan, she recently moved to Colorado to be close to the mountains, which still take her breath away every single day.